has no right to rob fu... interest, inspiration and ... from contact with anim... vation is necessary because it is from mammal sources that we can help to feed the world's ever-increasing population.

Mammal species have been reduced to a dangerously low level through Man's greed and arrogance. Unfortunately, only a small minority of people in the world as yet understand the need for conservation.

As conservationists we should adopt the following basic rules:

Preserve the habitat of mammal species and never disrupt it without undertaking conservation measures.

Maintain an adequate breeding stock, particularly of those animals which we hunt or exploit in other ways.

See to it that no mammal is killed or persecuted without a very good reason.

Malabar Civet

Contents

Disappearing Mammals

by
JOHN LEIGH-PEMBERTON

Publishers: Ladybird Books Ltd . Loughborough
© Ladybird Books Ltd 1973
Printed in England

Loss of habitat

As well as food and water, every animal requires a place in which to live. This is known as the animal's 'habitat' and varies according to the type of animal and the way in which it has evolved over millions of years. Animals are capable of adapting themselves, in varying degrees, to new habitats but as a rule this takes a very long time.

A species deprived of its habitat, particularly if this happens suddenly, will not breed readily and will eventually die out. A forest species cannot suddenly adapt itself to desert life, and tree-dwellers cannot suddenly convert to existence on a marsh or steppe.

All over the world habitats are being destroyed or altered by the activities of Man. Seldom is any thought given to the species for whom the habitat provides a home. When marshes are drained the marshland wild life comes to an end. When a forest is felled for its timber, or in order to convert the land to agricultural use, the animal inhabitants of that forest disappear just as do the trees.

A good example of this occurs in Madagascar, home of the lemurs, unique primates found nowhere else in the world other than the nearby Comoro Islands. Twenty-one lemur species, including Coquerel's mouse-lemur and the very rare Forsyth-Major's sifaka, are facing extinction through the destruction of their forest habitat.

French zoologists, in conjunction with the World Wildlife Fund, have established a lemur sanctuary on the Madagascan island of Nossi-Mangabé.

Coquerel's mouse-lemur *(above)*
Forsyth-Major's sifaka *(below)*

4

0 7214 0342 5

Loss of habitat due to cultivation of wild places

The wild places of the world are gradually disappearing. Man is taking them over and converting them to his own use. Whenever this happens a sequence of events takes place which disrupts the whole of the wild life pattern.

The cultivation of wild places means that habitats are altered and the animals and birds which live there disappear. A sort of 'chain-reaction' is produced which involves mammals, birds, reptiles, insects, plants, the soil—even the weather itself.

If, for instance, an African forest is cleared, the plants upon which antelopes feed disappear; so do the antelopes; and so do the animals, such as lions, which prey upon the antelopes. Other predators may become too numerous or may begin preying upon livestock. Traps and poisons, introduced to control these 'pests', inevitably harm other forms of life. In fact, all species suffer—not just a few.

In the United States, prairie dogs once lived in burrows and occupied huge areas in the prairie. They were preyed upon (and controlled) by other meat-eaters (carnivores) such as the black-footed ferret. With the coming of land cultivation the prairie dogs—members of the squirrel family—almost disappeared, having been poisoned, trapped and deprived of their habitat. Always a rare animal, the black-footed ferret is also now almost extinct. Such a sequence of events may be inevitable, but it provides an example of how and why species can disappear.

By establishing prairie dog reserves in National Parks, into which the black-footed ferret can be introduced, it is hoped to save both species.

Black-footed ferret *(above)*
Utah prairie dog *(below)*

Lòss of habitat due to overgrazing by domestic animals

Fewer than two hundred Kashmir stags remain in the world. These magnificent, once numerous deer live in a special sanctuary at Dachigam in Kashmir. It might be thought that there they would be safe from the poachers and 'sportsmen' who so drastically reduced their numbers in the past. But this supposedly safe area is now invaded by sheep and cattle in such numbers that the Kashmir stag (or hangul as it is sometimes called) is driven from its feeding ground.

This over-grazing by domestic stock presents conservationists with a difficult problem. No sooner is a reserve established to preserve some threatened species than the local inhabitants move in their flocks, thereby making the reserve ineffective. Even gorillas are similarly threatened, as are many forms of deer, antelope and wild goat such as markhor. Not only grazing land is affected; in the Gobi Desert the domestic herds and flocks are driving the extremely rare Przewalski's horse from the very limited water supplies, thereby contributing to its approaching extinction as a wild animal.

As well as taking food and water from wild grazing mammals, domestic stock also introduce diseases which can kill off whole colonies of rare species. The rare Indian wild ass and many antelope and wild cattle throughout the world are threatened by such diseases.

Wild animals, often migratory and controlled naturally by predators, never over-graze their habitat. Domestic animals, especially sheep and goats, tend to do so; and habitats are very slow to recover from the damage they do.

8   **Kashmir stag**

How the human population explosion reacts against mammals

The cultivation of wild places for crops or stock-raising, and the consequent destruction of animal habitats, have occurred mainly as a result of the rapid increase in the world's human population. Human beings demand more and more space and rely increasingly on their ability to exploit the natural world in order to sustain their ever-increasing numbers.

Some areas of the world are particularly affected by this process. In South America men carve their way into the vast jungles. Mammal species, only recently discovered, are being pushed out of existence before we can discover anything about them. The same pressures exist in India and in Europe, where there is no longer space for such animals as the wolf or the bear to survive.

The problem is at its worst in south-east Asia, where the population explosion has been overwhelming. Everywhere there is terrible poverty and ignorance, and the pressure on wild life and wild places has become irresistible. Mammal species are deprived of habitat or are exploited in every possible way. Almost all mammals, including monkeys and leopards, are considered suitable as food, and many species are on the verge of extinction.

Among these are the Sumatran and Javan species of rhinoceros, of which the Javan is the rarer. Fewer than fifty of the latter exist today, although their numbers are at present stable. But it seems unlikely that the Javan rhinoceros can survive for long unless a prosperous breeding stock can be established in the reserve set aside for them at Udjung Kulon in Java. An intensive study project is at present in progress in an attempt to bring this about.

Javan rhinoceros

The ruthless demands of the fur trade

It is hard to believe that some animals can become rare simply because they are beautiful. Yet this is true of many animals whose fur or wool is sought after for fashion purposes. Throughout the centuries men and women have adorned themselves with the fur of mammals, particularly the flesh-eating animals. During the last two hundred years this practice has grown so much that the very existence of many species is threatened.

Some of the principal victims have been the foxes, martens, fishers, otters and sables. They have been trapped, poisoned, shot or put to death by other and often terribly brutal methods—not in order to provide warmth but solely to meet the demands of fashion.

During the present century great damage has been done to the cat family. All those with striped or spotted coats have been hunted until about ten species have been put in danger of extinction. These include the tiger, clouded leopard, jaguar, leopard and ocelot. The beautiful snow leopard, a unique animal of the Asian mountain ranges, is now gravely threatened. Always rare, the number remaining is now estimated to be certainly no more than a thousand. Although legally protected throughout its range, the very high price still paid for skins attracts poachers and unlawful traders.

So long as women are prepared to wear coats made from these furs, the trade will continue until the supply runs out because the animals themselves have become extinct.

Snow leopard

More about the fur trade

Flesh-eating animals are not the only mammals which have suffered from the activities of the fur trade. Beavers, both European and Canadian, have for centuries provided beautiful, soft fur which has the double attraction of being warm as well as fashionable. Not yet in danger of extinction, the beaver is now a much rarer animal than in the past.

Fur seals have been so ruthlessly hunted that laws have had to be passed to protect them. The numbers are now increasing, but some species have been made extremely rare. The same story can be told of the sea otter, once almost extinct but now, happily, increasing. In Australia the koala had to be protected because of the terrible effect on it of the fur trade earlier in this century. Monkey fur, particularly that of the black and white colobus monkey from Africa, was also once much in demand.

The chinchilla, a very pretty rodent from the Andes, is now almost extinct in the wild, due entirely to over-hunting by greedy trappers who would not even allow the animal a breeding season. Chinchillas are now bred extensively on fur farms, but this does not repair the damage done to the wild stock.

Also in the Andes, the vicuna, a member of the camel family, has become threatened. For centuries the wild herds were rounded-up every two years, shorn of their superb wool and then released. Today the vicuna is callously slaughtered in order to obtain the whole skin as easily as possible. The number of vicunas is now one tenth that of twenty years ago.

Vicuna *(above)* **Chinchilla** *(below)*

The killing of animals for food

It would be difficult to name any species of animal which has not been eaten somewhere in the world, at some time or other. People eat monkeys and manatees, leopards, rats and whales. Even anteaters and armadillos are considered delicacies in South America. In Madagascar, lemurs and the rare falanouc are favoured.

However, the hoofed animals form the main source of food. In the past the balance between demand and supply has been fairly satisfactory. But two factors have now arisen which have altered the whole situation. The human population explosion has increased the demand for meat, while the loss of habitat has reduced the supply. Moreover, methods of killing are now much more effective; the modern rifle, available throughout the world, has replaced the less efficient bow, spear and boomerang.

The numbers of deer, wild cattle, antelopes, wild pigs, horses, asses, sheep and goats are, therefore, getting less and less, a situation which will surely get worse as the human population grows. Inevitably in Asia and Africa these mammal species will disappear needlessly because they will be slaughtered without thought of conservation. And yet, properly managed, the stocks of wild animals could provide a continuing source of meat.

A typical example of what could happen in the future is provided by the almost total disappearance of the black-faced impala, a sub-species found until recently in south-west Africa. Unprotected by the enforcement of game laws, it has been ceaselessly hunted by the Africans, to most of whom the idea of conservation is unknown.

Black-faced impala

Destructive hunting —1

Many mammals of the Arctic are facing the problem of changing climatic conditions. It is estimated that by the end of the century the Arctic ocean will be ice-free in summer and that the whole Arctic region will be warmer. This will have a profound effect on mammals such as the polar bear and reindeer, which depend upon the ice to make migration possible.

The polar bear and the beautiful white reindeer from Novaya Zemlya also have to face the dangers of Man's hunting activities. There is no doubt that hunting is the deadliest of all the forces which mammals have to face. It occurs throughout the world, all too often carried out without any regard for conservation.

The Novaya Zemlya reindeer is hunted for its skin, flesh and antlers. The polar bear is also hunted by Eskimos, fur-traders and seal hunters. But by far the worst form of polar bear hunting is that practised in Alaska under the name of sport. There the polar bear is shot from ski-planes or helicopters by anyone with a licence who is sufficiently rich, callous, stupid or un-sporting enough to do so. Laws have been passed to secure some measure of protection for polar bears, and a breeding reserve has been established for them on Wrangel Island in the USSR. But like all conservation laws, these are almost impossible to enforce and the animal remains in some danger of extinction.

Polar bear *(above)*
Novaya Zemlya reindeer *(below)*

...s of hunting, that which is solely for
...e the most destructive. A species can
...ved from possible extinction if it is con-
...orting purposes; but, throughout most of
...nting and conservation are not combined.
...t is only in recent times that this idea of
...tion for the purpose of hunting has been
...duced.

Since the improvement in the design of fire-arms, dating from the early nineteenth century, the ability of Man to destroy other species has greatly increased. It was during the nineteenth century that the idea of 'big-game hunting' developed. The rarer and more splendid an animal, the more it was sought after as a trophy. Stags with the finest antlers, elephants with the heaviest tusks, lions with the biggest manes, were all eagerly sought. It was assumed that the supply was inexhaustible and that Man had every right to plunder nature.

A notable example is provided by the fate of the Asian lion—an animal which once ranged from Asia Minor to Persia and India. It was hunted almost to extinction by British military personnel during the nineteenth century. Thousands were slaughtered, the finest specimens being reserved for Indian princes and distinguished visitors.

Fewer than two hundred lions are left in all Asia; they are found only in the Gir forest in the state of Gujarat, India. The increased intrusion of domestic cattle into this area has driven off the lion's natural prey such as deer and wild pig. Thus the declining numbers, persecuted by local farmers, have little chance of recovery. Now, perhaps too late, protective measures have been introduced.

Asian lion

Destructive hunting—3

A species does not become endangered when hunted to a limited extent under sensibly controlled conditions which allow a close season for breeding purposes. In the past, native populations throughout the world, equipped with primitive weapons, made little impact on the numbers of the animals they hunted. The human population was small compared with what it is today; its demands for food and the damage it could do were far less.

The whole picture has changed. Today, a vastly increased human race, of which parts are often desperately poor and hungry, has highly efficient weapons.

An animal such as the Arabian oryx, once hunted by men on horseback armed with spears, now has to face men in jeeps armed with automatic weapons. The Bedouin, who have always hunted the oryx, have been joined by the staff of European and American oil companies. As a result the Arabian oryx, as a wild animal, now numbers no more than a few hundred.

However, in this case a magnificent and heartening effort at conservation has been achieved. In 1962 the Fauna Preservation Society, with help from the World Wildlife Fund, instituted 'Operation Oryx'. This resulted in the establishment of a small breeding herd at Phoenix Zoo, Arizona, where the climate somewhat resembles that of the oryx's natural habitat in southern Arabia. The small herd has prospered, and there is now every hope that this species can be rescued from extinction.

Unfortunately it is not every species of rare mammal which can be rescued in this way. Many fail to adapt themselves or do not breed in captivity.

Arabian oryx

Exploitation for trade—1

The exploitation of mammal species for profit has had the most disastrous results. No other single cause has contributed so much towards the extinction of animal species.

We have already read of the damage done to many animals by the fur trade; but many other mammals have been terribly persecuted entirely because of Man's greed, thoughtlessness or ignorance. The ruthless hunting of all five species of rhinoceros, simply to obtain the horn for its supposed medicinal qualities, is an obvious instance.

However, by far the most serious example is the damage done by the whaling industry. Whaling is carried out almost exclusively by the so-called civilised nations, who have invested huge sums of money in building and equipping whaling fleets. The methods of the whalers are highly efficient and very cruel. As a result of their activities, five species of whale are in danger of extinction and five more are very rare. As one species declines in number another is hunted to keep the trade going.

The blue whale, the largest mammal that has ever lived, is in grave danger of extinction. But, like other rare whales, it is still hunted in spite of international agreements and protective laws which are inadequate and impossible to enforce.

Oil, whalebone (baleen) and bone are obtained from whales. These products are manufactured into margarine, soap, cosmetics and fertilisers. Whale meat is eaten in some countries, and it is also in great demand for the manufacture of tinned pet-foods. Each of these products can be produced from alternative sources, and there is no justification for the continuance of the totally destructive practice of whaling.

Blue whale

Exploitation for trade—2

For hundreds of years, all seals have been persecuted and commercially exploited. As man discovered the more remote parts of the world he found new species of seals or sea lions which could supply flesh, fur, hide and bone. Until very recently the annual killing of various species totalled many hundreds of thousands. This killing was not controlled by any kind of conservation laws and was frequently very brutal.

Seals come ashore and congregate in large colonies in order to breed. They move awkwardly on land and their pups, in particular, are quite helpless. Approaching them is therefore a simple matter and over-killing becomes all too easy. Both in the Arctic and Antarctic waters many species were seriously reduced in number, although since the introduction of conservation laws there has been some improvement. This applies to the northern fur seal of which there is now an estimated population of over three million. The number was once fewer than one hundred thousand.

The walrus is still seriously over-hunted and its numbers continue to fall.

Little is known about the breeding of seals in captivity, and conservation of rare species by this means seems to be very unlikely.

Other mammals are killed for trade on a smaller scale. These include civets and musk deer, whose glands produce substances much used in the manufacture of perfumes. Rhinoceros are killed for their horn; tigers for their blood, bones and whiskers. Wapiti were once killed just for their teeth, and wildebeest for their tails. Almost always the carcases were left to rot.

Walrus *(above)* **Northern fur seal** *(below)*

Deliberate destruction

From earliest times Man has managed to kill off, by various means, whole species of animals from certain areas. He has done this in self-defence or for the protection of his environment, his crops or his herds. As the means of destruction became more efficient (for instance, the development of fire-arms) more and more species were affected.

When Man changed from a hunting creature to an agricultural creature, species such as deer, which had once been valuable to him as food, became a nuisance to his crops and competed with his grazing stock for food. This happened throughout Europe in the Middle Ages and was repeated in North America during the eighteenth and nineteenth centuries.

In North America the cattle-men fought a long war against the grizzly bear, the wolf, the coyote and the cougar. Now sixteen sub-species of grizzly bear are extinct and the red wolf is almost so. The gray wolf has left much of its former territory, and only the cleverer and more adaptable coyote has survived in any numbers.

Of course, deliberate destruction of species which threaten Man's existence goes on throughout the world. Many species have been seriously reduced in number in Australia, and in Asia almost all wild animals of any size are classed as enemies. Throughout its enormous range, from South Africa to Siberia, the leopard is killed not only for its skin but because it threatens sheep and cattle.

This attitude towards mammals is one of the greatest difficulties which conservationists have to face. The need for the preservation of wild life must be understood and made acceptable to those who live in contact with it.

Grizzly bear *(above)* **Red wolf** *(below)*

The use of animals for medical research

There will always be differences of opinion as to the extent to which animals should be used in medical research. There are perhaps two conclusions which everyone who studies the subject can accept. Firstly, that great knowledge has been obtained, and much human suffering avoided by this practice. Secondly, that much of the use of animals by researchers could be considered wasteful, and has often caused needless suffering to the animals involved.

Conservationists are concerned with the effect that the use of animals in medical research can have upon species which, for other reasons, may already be reduced in numbers.

As populations expand and as education becomes available on an ever increasing scale, more and more research institutes are certain to be set up all over the world. This may well happen in countries where, as yet, the need for intelligent conservation of mammal species is not understood. The resultant ruthless use of wild animals for medical research might then become so great as to have a really damaging effect on wild life.

Today, thousands of animals are bought every year by medical research institutes, some from animal traders whose methods of capture are extremely questionable. In particular, monkeys—so similar to Man in many ways—are used in enormous numbers.

The great apes, particularly the gorilla and chimpanzee, are already in some danger because of the demands of research institutes. Incredibly, it has been even seriously suggested by some medical men that gorillas could supply hearts for transplants to human patients.

The effects of deadlier weapons

The nineteenth century saw a marked advance in the development and perfection of fire-arms. Both for military and sporting purposes, range, accuracy, hitting power and ease of handling were improved. Perhaps the most important improvement came about in 1861 with the invention of breech-loading guns using a cartridge. Up till then men had used muzzle-loaders, almost useless in wet weather and very slow in reloading.

This improvement in weapons was really a very important event in the history of the decline of both mammal and bird species. Almost at once it became possible for men to kill animals more easily. Nor were the improved fire-arms confined to Europe and America. During the next hundred years they spread all over the world.

Today, native populations in the so-called underdeveloped countries hunt with rifles instead of spears and bows. The animals which they have always hunted throughout history, already declining from other causes, are now being wiped out at an alarming rate.

The addax is a remarkable antelope found in the Sahara. It is a slow mover and offers a simple target to the mounted tribesmen armed with rifles, who hunt it for meat and skin. The idea of conservation simply does not occur to these hunters, and the laws which exist to protect the addax cannot be enforced. No reserve exists at present and its complete extinction seems a certainty.

This sad story could be told of many other species in the same area, where almost the whole mammal population is threatened, not least through the spread of fire-arms among people who use them irresponsibly.

Addax

More about the effects of deadlier weapons

In all Arab countries, from the Atlas mountains eastwards as far as Persia, the number of wild mammals has declined sharply over the past fifty years. Some species, like the Atlas bear and the Barbary lion, are already extinct, and the leopards and hyaenas of the area are now extremely rare.

But the species most reduced in number are the gazelles, deer and antelopes. Ten different races of gazelle are now in danger, due almost entirely to hunting of a needless and often illegal kind. This hunting has been carried out on an enormous scale, not only by local herdsmen and tribesmen armed with modern rifles, but also by foreigners, often the employees of oil companies from Europe and America, who have set an appalling example. Gazelles, once hunted sportingly with hounds and falcons, have been slaughtered in thousands by automatic weapons mounted on jeeps and even aircraft.

At the same time the whole area has been affected by troops engaged in various conflicts. In Morocco and Algeria, Saudi Arabia, Jordan and Israel, the military have used their modern weapons to do incredible harm. Protective laws are useless, for the areas are so vast and remote that supervision is impossible.

The very rare Persian fallow deer has also been drastically hunted. Meanwhile its habitat—the wooded banks of rivers—has been affected by tree felling and the intrusion of cattle.

Fortunately, many hoofed animals seem well suited to rescue by the establishment of captive breeding herds in suitable areas. So the gazelles, the Persian fallow deer and the addax may be saved in the same way that the Arabian oryx has been.

Goitered gazelle *(above)*
Persian fallow deer *(below)*

Killing for superstition

All over the world, Man has always had superstitions about animals. We say that black cats are lucky, or that it is unlucky to look at the tail of a pie-bald horse. Although we may not believe such superstitions, in some parts of the world the supposed magical properties of animals are taken very seriously.

Most eastern people believe that the horn of rhinoceros produces virility and fertility. All over the East there is still a ready sale, at high prices, for powdered rhinoceros horn. Very largely as a result of this belief all five species of rhinoceros are very rare, particularly in Asia.

Eastern people also believe that the blood, bones and whiskers of tigers have medicinal value. They are supposed to impart courage, cure rheumatism and ward off ghosts.

The gall-stones or bezoars produced by animals such as the ibex are thought to have medicinal and magical properties. So are the antlers of the Sika deer. The foals of the rare Persian wild ass or onager are believed to produce bile which can cure eye diseases.

The aye-aye, a lemur found only in Madagascar and one of the rarest mammals, was at one time regarded by the natives as a witch. They treated it with respect, even leaving out food for it; to kill it was forbidden. Nowadays, quite the reverse is true—the aye-aye is supposed to foretell death, which can only be avoided by killing it.

It is easy to dismiss these superstitions as trivial nonsense. But, added to other causes, they can contribute towards the decline in numbers of the species concerned.

Aye-aye

The menace of pollution

One of the main problems which all conservationists have to face is that of Man's pollution of his own habitat. This vast subject includes sewage disposal, the effects of oil, insecticides, fertilisers and the dumping of dangerous and poisonous matter. Pollutants include smoke, exhaust fumes, and industrial and domestic waste. These threats to life of all kinds are, of course, increased as the human population grows.

Other species cannot escape from this man-made pollution. The poisons employed to destroy weeds or insect pests eventually affect all forms of life. Rivers and estuaries are fouled by sewage and industrial waste, and the birds, fishes and mammals which live there are killed or denied a habitat. The sea, now increasingly used as a dumping ground for poisonous waste, is becoming polluted. Creatures such as plankton and krill (the food of many other forms of life) are destroyed.

All over the world habitats are ruined by industrial waste, cement dust, slag-heaps and rubbish dumps. Even in the Arctic the fall-out from atomic testing has affected the moss upon which reindeer feed, and radio-active poisons collect in the reindeer's bones.

Oil-slicks are a special menace. For instance, the Californian sea otter, recently saved from near-extinction due to over-hunting, now faces the problem of oil on its marine habitat. Sea otters have no protective layer of fat or blubber, as seals do, and depend upon their fur to maintain a blanket of warm air round them. If this becomes oiled and waterlogged they are liable to die of exposure.

Sea otter

The cost of 'progress'

Men build roads and railways, dams, power-stations and bridges. To do so they alter the landscape and erect fences upon it. All these activities are necessary, but they affect, often seriously, the lives and even the survival of the animals which live in the area.

A huge lake, artificially created to power a hydro-electric scheme, can obviously have widespread effects. This has happened in Africa and in Australia and generally many species have suffered as a result. Railways too, destroy habitats, although quite often railway embankments form a new sort of refuge for some creatures. Dams and bridges change the character of rivers, and then animals such as otters and beavers suffer. Fences, especially electric fences (as used in North Africa) alter migratory routes and cut off feeding areas. So do oil pipe-lines, as has been found in Alaska. Here, the oil companies are taking great pains to ensure that the migratory routes of the caribou are unaffected by oil pipe-lines.

But perhaps the greatest threat of this kind is the construction of more and more roads, and the increase in the number of cars that use them. It would be impossible to total the numbers of wild mammals (to say nothing of birds) killed annually by cars. Nocturnal animals, in particular, are at special risk.

The very attractive Kaibab squirrel is found only on the Kaibab Plateau, Grand Canyon, Arizona. It has never learned to live with the motor car and many are killed each year on the roads—increasing the danger of extinction of this already rare species.

Kaibab squirrel

The animal victims of war

During the past fifty years, many wars have done increasing damage to the whole environment. Not only the opposing armies, but all forms of life have become involved. Extremely destructive weapons have wiped out towns, diverted rivers, destroyed forests and scarred the surface of the earth.

The effect on mammal life has been severe, and has endangered the continued existence of many species.

The wars of twenty years ago in North Africa, and the more recent ones in Israel, Arabia and Tibet, have resulted in wild places being occupied by military units. Either in an attempt to 'live off the land' or for 'sport', these armed forces have killed such animals as antelope, yak, gazelle, ibex, deer and wild asses. In the Congo, the United Nations forces and the Congolese Army did untold damage to the wild life, killing thousands of animals including rare antelopes and even gorillas.

In Vietnam, the use of napalm and defoliants (which kill all vegetation) have devastated huge areas which provided habitats for many species. Some of these animals, already rare, are most unlikely to recover in number. We shall never be able to assess the damage done to wild life by bombardment and chemical warfare.

The kouprey, a magnificent forest ox, was discovered in Cambodia in 1937. It is estimated that there are no more than two hundred of them and that the number is decreasing. In view of the extensive destruction of habitat caused by the wars in Indo-China, the chances of survival for the kouprey must be slight indeed.

The sad consequences of the pet trade

The golden-headed tamarin is an extremely rare marmoset found occasionally in a small area of Brazil. It is one of a number of similar species which are in great demand as pets, particularly in the United States.

Pet shops rely on animal dealers for their supplies, and very often these traders are quite unscrupulous in their methods of capture. In fact, for every one marmoset delivered to the pet shop about four die when captured, or on the journey afterwards.

Like many other small and attractive mammals, marmosets, even if they survive, do not breed readily in captivity. Thus as pets they only lessen the numbers of a species which may already be rare.

All too common is the desire to possess, as a pet, an animal which is exotic or unusual. But catching such a pet quite possibly involves needless destruction and great cruelty. Moreover its possession means that the species is reduced and not conserved.

Monkeys, small cats such as margays, exotic squirrels, miniature deer, otters, foxes, galagoes and many other mammals are caught, transported (some dying because of the dreadful travelling conditions) and traded all over the world. Many are very difficult to keep in captivity and soon die. This fact does not worry some pet shop owners—they can supply others.

Conservationists are concerned with stocks of wild animals in their natural habitat. The keeping of individual wild animals as pets has no place in conservation. In any case there are many domestic animals suitable as satisfactory and rewarding pets.

Golden-headed tamarin

Collection for zoos, menageries and safari parks

Zoos and menageries used to be considered no more than collections of caged wild animals shown in parks or gardens for the entertainment of visitors. This mistaken viewpoint is often still held, despite the great change that has taken place among civilised people in their attitude towards mammals. All over the world zoos exist which are little better than concentration camps for animals.

The ideal zoo is one which does not take animals from the wild state but breeds its own stocks. It works to conserve and to breed rare species, and carries out research into animal health and welfare. No menageries, and few safari parks and zoos can claim to reach this standard.

The irresponsible collection of wild animals for exhibition results in injury, shock, death, reduction of the species and wastage of wild life. Now that we can visit reserves or see animals on film or television, there is no good reason for the existence of these less responsible zoos. It is said that these places give pleasure to thousands and increase the general interest in animals, but too many species are in danger of disappearance to justify any further plundering by commercially-minded animal collectors.

Facing possible extinction because of this activity is the orang-utan. To obtain a young specimen from the jungle, several adults may have to be killed by collectors who are often little better than poachers. Often the young orang-utan dies before it reaches its destination, and yet another destructive attempt at capture is then made.

Multiple dangers

In this book we are shown some of the reasons why mammal species become rare or extinct. One single cause is generally not enough to wipe out a whole species, but it must be remembered that the rate of breeding decreases to a dangerously low level if numbers are reduced below a certain point.

Usually it is a combination of causes which does the damage. The destruction of habitat added to over-hunting and food shortage, soon results in a species being threatened. Persecution during the breeding season and collecting for zoos or pet shops can very quickly have the same effect.

A species can very easily be wiped out on islands, where the animal populations cannot be replaced naturally. This is happening in places like Formosa, Madagascar and Java. But even on continents the number of threats to the lives of mammals has increased so suddenly that there is often the same grave situation.

Having a large range and no natural enemies, tigers might be thought to be safe. Yet now they are in grave danger of extinction wherever they live. Already rare, the huge, long-haired tigers of Manchuria and Siberia, for instance, face a combination of threats. They are hunted as zoo specimens, for fur, for medicine and for sport. In China they are deliberately destroyed. Their natural prey is becoming scarcer and their territories and habitats are diminishing. What hope is there for any species which has to face so many disadvantages?

Siberian tiger

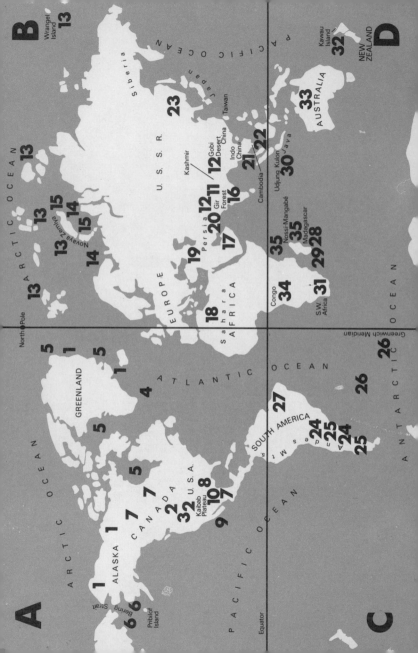